LEGENDS A
OF I

By R. S. Holland

BRADWELL
BOOKS

Published by Bradwell Books

9 Orgreave Close Sheffield S13 9NP

Email: books@bradwellbooks.co.uk

British Library Cataloguing in Publication Data: a catalogue record for this book is available from the British Library.

1st Edition

ISBN: 9781910551004

Print: Berforts Information Press. Eynsham. OX29 4JB

Design by: Andrew Caffrey

Typesetting by: Mark Titterton

Photograph Credits: IStock and the author

Cover Photographs
Background image: Shutterstock/ Panos Karas
Green man image: Shutterstock/ Gwoeii
Stonehenge:©English Heritage

CONTENTS

IStock Photo

Salisbury Cathedral is one of Wiltshire's most iconic buildings and a number of strange traditions belong to it.

INTRODUCTION

The folklore and folk tales of the British Isles make for an endlessly fascinating study. A glorious confusion of ancient beliefs has evolved over the millennia thanks to the many different races that have settled here. In England they have included Stone Age and Bonze Age tribes, the Iron Age Celts, Romans, Angles, Saxons, Norsemen and Normans.

Into this cultural melting pot have been thrown any number of superstitions and half-remembered tales of cultural heroes, some real, some mythical, and many a mixture of both.

Our ancestors lived very different lives to those we enjoy today. Most were tied to the land and had an intimate relationship with the seasons and the natural world. Few had travelled further than their nearest market town; many had never even strayed that far from the rustic landscape they knew so well.

Nevertheless, their seemingly limited existence was coloured with an awareness of another world, one where supernatural beings lived alongside them just out of sight; where illness or death could be brought about not by microbes but by witchcraft; where familiar landmarks took on mystical significance. Heroes and villains from a past age lived again in dramatic legends told down the generations, while neighbouring communities were ridiculed by village wits, who invented tall tales about their idiocy and gullibility.

In this book you will be introduced to just a taster of the legends and folklore which enlivened the days and nights of Wiltshire

The Westbury Horse, or rather its predecessor, is said to have been created in 878 to celebrate King Alfred's decisive Battle of Ethandun against the Danes. The carving visible today was made in 1778, nine centuries years after the event.

country folk a century or more ago. You will learn strange superstitions about the county's celebrated ancient monuments; meet the Moonrakers, a flying monk, wicked highwaymen and even wickeder witches; encounter kings and knights, saints with magic powers, and the Devil, rather more frequently than one might wish. Fairies too appear and ghosts, like the infamous Demon Drummer, lurk among its pages.

The folklore of Wiltshire paints the county as a wonderfully magical place. I hope you enjoy this brief tour through its wonders.

The 17th-century antiquarian John Aubrey
is responsible for recording a great deal of Wiltshire folklore.

STONEHENGE AND AVEBURY

Wiltshire is celebrated for its many impressive prehistoric monuments. The county has one of the largest concentrations of ancient burial mounds in England and numerous standing stones, hill forts and other earthworks dating from the depths of antiquity. It also boasts the two most famous stone circles in the world, Stonehenge and Avebury.

Stonehenge is an iconic structure, known the world over. Its brooding presence on Salisbury Plain has attracted strange tales to it for centuries, perhaps millennia. For thousands of years the complex of ditches and stone circles has survived, its original purpose long forgotten, a magnet for wonder and superstition. Before we get on to the folklore, it would be interesting to briefly consider the facts.

The earliest work on the structure that later became known as Stonehenge began at least 3,000 years ago, with the excavation of a circular ditch, 300 feet (100 metres) in diameter, with an inner and outer bank. However, there is evidence that a series of wooden 'totem poles' had stood here thousands of years before. The area may well have been used for sacred or ceremonial purposes for 10,000 years or more. Stones were erected about 500 years after the ditch – or henge – was dug. These consisted of two types of stone: massive blocks of 'sarsen stone', a kind of sandstone found locally, and much smaller 'blue stones' which chemical analysis has identified as having come all the way from Pembrokeshire in South Wales.

The origin of the blue stones is particularly enigmatic. Had they really come from South Wales, or had they perhaps been found as 'erratics', dropped in the area by glacial activity at the end of the Ice Age? Blue stones have been found nowhere else in England, used in prehistoric monuments or otherwise. There

Stonehenge, Wiltshire's most famous ancient monument. One of the small, mysterious blue stones can be seen to the right of centre, leaning at an angle between the massive sarsen stones.

must have been something very special about them indeed. They are dwarfed by the circle and separate horseshoe of mighty sarsens. The sarsen stones are particularly impressive thanks to their having been set up as 'trilithons', that is to say, two uprights capped by a single recumbent stone. The expertise required by prehistoric people to not only raise stones 13 feet (4 metres) high but to then position horizontal blocks on top of them is mind-boggling.

Initially the blue stones were arranged in a double arc but two or three centuries later they were rearranged, twice, to form their present arrangement of circle and horseshoe. In the meantime, massive entrance stones had been raised, as well as four 'station stones' outside the circle. A track was also constructed down to the River Avon.

After Stonehenge was built, it attracted the interest of later waves of prehistoric settlers and they set up burial mounds all around it. The monument appears to have been in use for thousands of years. Four of the larger stones have shapes resembling Bronze Age axes carved into them, showing that Stonehenge was still important 1,500 years after it was built. There is also evidence that it was still being used for ritual purposes by the Romano-British people in the first few centuries after Christ.

But what went on here? It's still a mystery. The only certainty is that, like other stone circles, Stonehenge could be used as a big seasonal clock. It has been aligned with the rising and setting of the sun on the shortest and longest days of the year. Significant lunar alignments have also been noted. Indeed, there appear to be dozens of alignments with various heavenly bodies, all helping a local community to plan sowing and harvest and ritually important days in the year.

Recent research suggests that Stonehenge was also used as a place of healing, a 'primeval Lourdes' as one commentator has put it. Archaeologist Mike Parker Pearson has also proposed a compelling theory linking another ancient site, Durrington Walls, with Stonehenge. In Dr Pearson's model, a ritual journey would be taken from the Durrington Walls via the River Avon to the place of the dead, represented by Stonehenge. It would seem that this enigmatic structure had many uses for our ancestors.

Intriguingly, two of the more recent theories regarding Stonehenge were both suggested by one of our oldest sources of information about the site. In the 12th century, the Welshman Geoffrey of Monmouth wrote his book *History of the Kings of Britain*, which is a treasure trove of British folklore and was largely responsible for popularising tales of King Arthur.

According to Geoffrey, Stonehenge was raised on Salisbury Plain by no less a personage than the wizard Merlin. In Geoffrey's account, the stones were erected during the reign of a king called Ambrosius Aurelianus, after whom Amesbury may be named. Ambrosius wished to commemorate a party of noblemen who had been treacherously killed at a feast some years previously and asked Merlin's advice on the matter. Merlin tells him of a circle of stones to be found at a mountain called Killaurus in Ireland. He names them the 'Dance of the Giants'.

'The stones be big,' says Merlin, 'nor is there stone anywhere without virtue. Even as they be now set up [in a circle], here shall they stand forever.'

The king laughs and asks why they should bother dragging over stones from Ireland, 'as if Britain were lacking in stones enough for the job?'

Merlin replies: 'Laugh not so lightly. In these stones is … a healing virtue against many ailments. Giants of old did carry them from the furthest ends of Africa and did set them up in Ireland what time they did inhabit there. Not a stone is there that lacketh in virtue of witchcraft.'

Here then we have a legend describing the stones' removal from a far place and of their possessing curative properties. This may well be a folk memory of the transportation of the enigmatic blue stones. The legend continues that Ambrosius's men struggled to topple and then transport the Dance of the Giants but that Merlin, laughing scornfully, constructed his own 'engines' to do the job and 'laid the stones down so lightly as none would believe'. His skill and cunning also helped him to see off opposition from the King of Ireland. Back in England, the stones were re-erected with equal ease, thanks to Merlin, in the same arrangement as they had stood in Ireland.

Another figure from folklore is also credited with creating Stonehenge: the Devil. The Devil is connected with many other ancient features in Wiltshire, as we shall see in regards to Avebury and in the next chapter. One tale, first recorded in the 18th century, has His Satanic Majesty transporting the stones from Ireland instead of Merlin. He bought the stones from an old Irish woman. Pouring a pile of gold coins in front of her, the Devil told the old woman he would pay her all she could gather from the pile while he took the stones over to England. But he cheated her: he flew back and forth so fast that the woman only had time to pick up one coin before the job was done.

Over on Salisbury Plain, the Devil re-erected the stones and then loudly boasted of his own cleverness, delighted that no one would know how the monument got to be there. However, he had been

The sun shines through Stonehenge's iconic trilithons. The monument's design helped its builders to identify important days of the year, such as midsummer and midwinter.

IStock Photo

observed by a travelling friar, who snorted out: 'That's what you think!' The Devil was so furious at having his prank spoiled, he lobbed an enormous stone at the friar and it caught him on the heel. The stone bears the impression of a heel and is still known as the Heel Stone today. Anyone standing within the circle will see the sun rise behind the Heel Stone on the summer solstice. A variant of this story combines both accounts of the building of Stonehenge. Merlin brings the monument over from Ireland but is struck on the heel by a stone thrown by the Devil, who is jealous of his handiwork.

Another folk belief regarding Stonehenge is that it is impossible to accurately count all its stones and bad luck to try. This is a common superstition found at many stone circles around the British Isles. The antiquarian William Stukeley already knew of this superstition when he made his detailed investigation of Stonehenge in the 18th century. When he published his report, he quipped: 'Behold the solution of the mighty problem, the magical spell is broke, which has so long perplexed the vulgar. They think 'tis an ominous thing to count the true number of the stones, and whoever does so, shall certainly die after it.'

Equally important as Stonehenge, and indeed larger, is the stone circle complex at Avebury. This consists of a deep and extensive henge (i.e. a ditch and embankment) surrounding the remains of one large circle and two smaller ones. In addition, there are the remnants of two 'avenues' of stones leading into and out of the henge. Only two stones remain of the south-westerly avenue, but the south-easterly one still has numerous pairs of stones in situ. This more complete avenue originally wound its way up to a now lost complex of stones which bore the evocative name of the Sanctuary. The entire Avebury complex was built by Stone Age people and is even older than Stonehenge.

*An illustration in a medieval manuscript
showing Merlin building Stonehenge on Salisbury Plain.*

Little is known about what went on at Avebury. No doubt the circles could be used for astronomical dating purposes, as at Stonehenge, but beyond that it is conjecture. Some sort of lengthy ritual is suggested by the presence of the avenues, down which people could process into the stone circles and back out again. The depth of the henge is reminiscent of a castle moat and has placed the stone circles in splendid isolation, enhancing the sense of a sacred space. A recent theory has it that the outer bank of the henge was used as a vantage point to observe whatever rituals

The prehistoric standing stones at Avebury remain evocative today and suggested a number of superstitions to our ancestors.

went on inside the circles; in other words it resembled a Roman amphitheatre.

Remarkably, there is no recorded legend to account for the building of Avebury, by either human or supernatural agency. One or two of the stones do have traditions attached to them, however. One of the large diamond-shaped monoliths is said to cross the road at midnight and another is known as the Devil's Chair because it contains a hollow which forms a rough seat. The Devil is also linked to a pair of especially massive stones now called The Cove. An older name for them was the Devil's Brandirons. The two remaining stones of the south-westerly avenue are now best known as Adam and Eve but they have also been called the Devil's Quoits. Quoits was a popular rural game in which horseshoes (usually) were thrown at pegs in the ground. In both cases the implication is that only the Devil, with his great strength, could have dumped them there. Such stories also present Satan as a giant.

In the medieval period a settlement began to appear near the stones and this grew into the village of Avebury. A number of the monoliths were pulled down and used for building material. The reason any remain standing today is that not everyone was prepared to incorporate such uncanny objects into their homes. It is a curious fact that many of the stones were deliberately toppled and buried where they lay, an extraordinary waste of quality building material. This campaign of removing the monoliths from sight took place off and on over many centuries. It's possible each burial was carried out as an act of penance or part of some pact with God, for the prehistoric stones would certainly be considered devilish by the clergy.

The toppling of each stone would have been a major undertaking, difficult and dangerous. Just how dangerous was ably demonstrated

In the heart of the Avebury complex can be found The Cove, formerly known as the Devil's Brandirons. The Devil is linked to a number of the standing stones at Avebury.

IStock Photo

LEGENDS & FOLKLORE OF WILTSHIRE

in the 1930s when a project was under way to restore the buried stones to their original positions. Beneath one of the monoliths – standing 10 feet (3 metres) in height and weighing 13 tons – was found the corpse of a man. The coins in his purse showed he had been crushed by the stone in the early 14th century. The unfortunate man was left where he lay by his colleagues, who presumably did not have the means to raise the massive stone again. This incident may have put an end to the destruction of the circle. There is evidence for a folk belief extending into the 19th century of a man having been crushed by a stone, showing that the accident had a profound effect on the medieval villagers.

Strange things have been reported from Avebury over the years. In her book *Moonrakings*, local author Edith Olivier recalled an odd experience of her own here. In the teens of the 20th century, Miss Olivier was driving from Devizes to Marlborough in the early evening when she decided to break her journey at Avebury. It was twilight when she arrived. As she pulled over, she noticed there were lights among the stones. She could also hear music and other sounds of a fair taking place. Not interested in revisiting the atmospheric site while such revelries were taking place, Miss Olivier changed her mind, turned her car around, and continued her journey to Marlborough.

After she arrived, she happened to mention that a fair was taking place at Avebury. She was told this could not be the case, that no fair had been held in the village for at least fifty years. This statement proved to be true. Miss Olivier had seen and heard a ghostly fair among the ancient stones.

An apparition of a different sort was seen many years later by a student at the Lackham School of Agriculture, Miss J.M. Dunn. She told a collector of local folk stories, the aptly named Kathleen

Wiltshire, that one starry night she was driving back from Swindon along the road which cuts through the stone circle when she had what she described as 'a most uncanny feeling'. She then saw, picked out in the bright moonlight, small figures among the stones. Miss Dunn was convinced that for an instant she had experienced a glimpse back to the time of the Ancient Britons, when mysterious rituals were carried out here. She pointed out that our prehistoric ancestors were much smaller than modern man. Not so very long ago, somebody experiencing the same vision would have called the diminutive figures 'fairies'.

MORE ANCIENT MONUMENTS

In addition to Stonehenge and Avebury, Wiltshire can boast many other impressive ancient monuments. Because of their pagan origins, a number of these have also come to be associated with the Devil in folk belief.

The remains of a Bronze Age chambered tomb at Fyfield Down near Marlborough has long been known as the Devil's Den. There is a tradition that it is impossible to remove its stones. Many farmers, it is said, have done their best to clear the field, never mind how many horses or oxen they employ to do so, but the task was always beyond them. Similar stories are told about prehistoric stones throughout the British Isles, an indicator of the superstitious dread they at one time inspired. In the 1920s, the story was in some way discredited when an amateurish attempt was made to restore the fallen stones to their original position. The result, still seen today, is striking but not necessarily accurate.

There are several, more unusual traditions associated with the Devil's Den. One states that the Den serves as a kennel for a supernatural dog which is white in colour but has blazing red eyes. Another is that if anyone pours water into hollows on the capstone, it will have vanished by morning because a demon residing here will have drunk it overnight. Perhaps the oddest is that the Devil, who is usually believed to have created such places, is actually trying to destroy this one. Every midnight he latches the stones up to four white oxen but, like the farmers mentioned above, His Satanic Majesty has no more success in removing them.

A large stone, possibly natural in origin, stands at the foot of the downs at East Knoyle, and it is said that it extends below ground to at least the same number of feet as is visible above. Again, there is a tradition of farmers attempting to remove it from the field, the task proving impossible. The Devil is once more credited with its presence, having dropped it on his way to building Stonehenge.

A further folk tale about the Devil's activities is associated with another natural feature, Cley Hill, near Marlborough. The Devil was fed up with the pious behaviour of the people of Devizes and he decided to bury the town and its inhabitants so that their prayers would no longer offend his pointy ears. He travelled to the West Country and there filled an enormous sack with clay. Slowly he made his way back, weighed down by his burden. Eventually, he reached Wiltshire and here encountered an old man on the road near Warminster. He asked the traveller how many miles there were to Devizes.

'That's just what I want to know myself,' replied the quick-thinking old man. 'I set out for Devizes when my beard was black and now it's grey, and I haven't got there yet.'

Disgusted with the whole business, the Devil emptied out his sack and stomped off to create mischief elsewhere. The resultant pile of clay became Cley Hill. Yarns of this sort are told about a number of places throughout England. In another version, the old man is a cobbler with a sack full of shoes needing repair. He pretends they are the shoes he has worn out trying to reach the place the Evil One is planning to bury. Although natural in origin, Cley Hill may have been singled out because it is crowned with prehistoric burial mounds and a hill fort.

Silbury Hill is entirely artificial and was built at approximately the same time as the Avebury stone circles, which it overlooks. Standing 130 feet (40 metres) in height, it is the largest man-made mound in Europe and is about the same size as an Ancient Egyptian pyramid and of similar age (the Great Pyramid of Giza was completed within decades of Silbury being constructed). Unlike the pyramids and most other prehistoric mounds in Britain, however, Silbury Hill contains no burial. Its function remains a mystery, beyond its belonging to a manufactured sacred landscape. Some believe it represents the swollen belly of an Earth Mother goddess.

The Devil's Den chambered tomb near Marlborough is the subject of many strange superstitions. © *Richard Holland*

The same tale told about Cley Hill is told about Silbury, that it was made from a gigantic lump of earth which, in this case, the Devil intended to dump on top of Marlborough. The 'priests of Avebury' defeated his plan, however, and he was forced to drop the earth. An alternative version describes Silbury as having been formed when the Devil scraped the mud off his shovel while digging another enigmatic prehistoric earthwork, Wansdyke (more of which later).

Many vain attempts to find a burial, and its associated treasure, within Silbury Hill have been carried out over the centuries. Their failure did nothing to suppress a persistent legend that the mound was raised over the tomb of an ancient ruler called King Zel (pronounced 'Sil' in the Wiltshire dialect). This mythical king was supposedly buried in the mound seated on a horse. Some accounts say he is clothed in golden armour. Other versions tell of his burial in a coffin of gold, or say that the horse and rider are in fact a life-sized statue of solid gold. All versions suggest the importance and wealth of the individual supposedly laid to rest here. There is no evidence that a person called Zel or Sil ever existed and he was probably made up to explain the name Silbury. Unfortunately, there is no clear indication of what 'sil' means either, and this remains just one of the many enigmas surrounding the colossal monument.

As an addition to the legend, Silbury Hill is said to be haunted by King Zel. His ghost rides his horse round the mound, dressed in golden armour. A headless figure is also supposed to be seen standing on the summit but its identity is a mystery.

We have already mentioned Wansdyke as having been constructed by the ubiquitous Devil. Wansdyke is a remarkable feature which runs for more than twenty miles (with a few gaps) from Hampshire, through Wiltshire to Somerset. It appears to be a massive defensive boundary consisting of a ditch and embankment, created in the 6th century. The name is a contraction of 'Woden's Dyke', after the chief god of the Anglo-Saxons. One old tradition states that the Devil carried out the work in just one day – a Wednesday. Wednesday is, of course, Woden's Day, and there is another tradition that Woden himself built the dyke, but that he too succeeded in doing so in a single day.

Returning to prehistory, we must consider the many ghostly stories told about some of the very many burial mounds to be found in Wiltshire. West Kennet Long Barrow is one of the most impressive in England and it belongs to the same prehistoric landscape which also includes Avebury and Silbury Hill. Built around 3600 BC, the barrow consists of several stone chambers covered in an earthen mound more than 300 feet (100 metres) long. The entrance to the tomb was sealed by massive 'blocking stones', but since excavations have been carried out it is now accessible. Recent archaeological evidence suggests that 46 people were buried here over a period lasting two or three decades but that the tomb remained open for at least a thousand years after they were placed in it. This suggests some form of ancestor worship, in which the dead are regularly visited and even removed to take part in community events. The sealing up of the tomb may have marked a change in religion.

The apparitions which tradition says haunt West Kennet Long Barrow are so mysterious they might themselves date from prehistoric times. The figure of a man, described as 'a priest', is said to enter the barrow on the longest day of the year – a significant day in the pagan calendar, as we have seen in relation to Stonehenge. The priest is followed into the tomb by a large white hound with red ears. Such dogs appear in fairy-lore throughout the UK. It's possible they represent a folk memory of an early breed

Silbury Hill towers over the Wiltshire landscape. This is another pre-Christian monument associated with the Devil, and it is also said to be haunted.

IStock Photo

of domestic dog. You may recall that a white dog also haunts the Devil's Den.

A burial mound at Vernditch has become confused with a traditional ghost story about a suicide. Suicide was considered self-murder, and those who had taken their own lives were banned from being buried in consecrated ground. In a practice dating back at least to Roman days, they were usually buried instead at crossroads, sometimes with a stake through their heart to prevent their spirits wandering. This particular barrow stands right by a crossroads. It is called Kit's Grave, a corruption of its old Anglo-Saxon name, but a tradition grew up that Kit was a young woman who had thrown herself into a well in the nearby churchyard. After burial, her sad spirit lingered round the mound. It is said the spot is so eerie that no birds will sing in its vicinity.

The West Kennet Long Barrow is even older than Stonehenge and Avebury and is haunted by two strange apparitions.

IStock Photo

Another ghost haunted a barrow on Roundway Down, near Devizes. The apparition would lead night-bound travellers to the mound and then vanish within it. After it was excavated in the 19th century, the ghost ceased to haunt. The opposite occurred at the Manton Barrow near Marlborough – the angry spirit of the person buried here thousands of years before took to wandering about after archaeologists took away her bones. The excavators discovered within the Manton Barrow the skeleton of an elderly woman ornamented with gold and amber jewellery. After the investigation, a woman living in the shadow of the barrow complained to her doctor that 'every night since that man came and disturbed the old creature, she did come out of the mound and walk around the house and "squinny" into the window. I do hear her most nights and want you to give me summat to keep her away.'

She presumably thought that the doctor, being an educated man, would know how to see off a ghost. Instead, he simply gave his troubled patient a strong sleeping draught. When he called on her several days later, she told him: 'The old creature came round the cottage as usual for a few nights but, not seeing me, gave up, thinking, no doubt, she had scared me away.'

Adam's Grave is another large long barrow, very prominent on the crest of Walker's Hill north of Alton Barnes. It faces Knap Hill, a Stone Age enclosure. Muriel Cobern was enjoying a ramble round the Downs here when something strange occurred. She explained what happened to Kathleen Wiltshire, who related it in her *Ghosts and Legends of the Wiltshire Countryside*. Miss Coburn was walking towards Adam's Grave when 'she suddenly felt very uneasy'.

'She glanced around,' continues Kathleen Wiltshire; 'it was very cloudy and rather cold, and no one else was about. A flock of sheep through which she was passing seemed untroubled, so she went on.

Suddenly, she could distinctly hear horses' hooves thudding, as if a whole army was coming at full gallop; but there was not a horse to be seen anywhere. Miss Cobern, walking much faster, she admits, passed Adam's Grave about a hundred yards to the right and then could hear the hooves no longer.'

Adam's Grave, on the summit of Walker's Hill, is a particularly large and prominent barrow. A phantom that is heard but not seen has been encountered here.
© *Richard Holland*

AN ENCOUNTER WITH THE FAIRIES

Throughout the British Isles, and further afield, there was for centuries a firm belief in a separate order of beings, human in appearance and customs, who regularly visited our world but were not part of it. Generically, they are known as the fairies.

The fairies of England took many forms. They might be as tiny as birds, a few feet tall or the same size as humans. They tended to wear a combination of green and red, but might be seen to adopt the myriad finery enjoyed by the human aristocracy.

It was considered sensible to always keep on the right side of the fairies; you never knew when one might be listening. For this reason they were sometimes referred to as 'the Good Neighbours'. They could be malicious or generous but more often they were simply amoral, their treatment of the humans they encountered depending entirely on the person's behaviour towards them. A few mortals enjoyed excellent relations with them but they were unpredictable, and swift to revenge supposed slights or disrespect.

What made them more dangerous was their continual campaign to inveigle people into their world, which they achieved by tempting them to join in one of their dances – fairies love dancing – or by promising a life of luxury and ease. This could prove fatal to their victims. Time runs at a different rate in fairyland. The dancing may seem to go on for a few pleasant hours, but in reality weeks, years or even centuries may pass by in the mortal world while it lasts. Fairy revels usually involved a feast after the dancing, but woe betide the mortal man or woman who joined in. By consuming fairy food and drink they became part of the fairy world and were unable to safely return to our world. Other fairies made efforts to steal human infants, and it was therefore important to baptise a new baby at the earliest opportunity.

Stories of adventures with the Good Neighbours, or references to places they were believed to hold their revels, are common in many English counties. There is, however, only one clear reference to a fairy encounter in Wiltshire. Fairies were popularly believed to inhabit burial mounds and to dance in ancient hill forts and enclosures, so this lack of tales seems surprising for such an archaeologically rich county as Wiltshire. The uncanny white hounds said to haunt the Devil's Den and West Kennet Long Barrow (see the 'More Ancient Monuments' chapter) could well be considered fairy dogs, but there is no other traditional fairy-lore attached to Wiltshire's ancient monuments. No doubt more tales of fairies were being whispered by Wiltshire firesides centuries ago but they have not come down to us.

The one undoubted fairy-haunted location we can point to in Wiltshire is Hackpen Hill, near Broad Hinton. Hackpen features one of the county's many white horse hill figures. These have been created by scraping the turf on the hillside to expose the white chalk beneath. None of the Wiltshire hill figures are of any great age (unlike the Uffington example in neighbouring Berkshire, which may well date back to the Iron Age), but several have replaced much older figures now only visible using hi-tech scanning devices. Hackpen Hill's white horse appears to be no older than the early 19th century and may have been dug to celebrate Queen Victoria's Coronation. Nevertheless, the hill itself has some antiquity. The

Old stories about little beings haunting the countryside can be found throughout the British Isles but they are rather scarce in Wiltshire.

ancient Ridgeway track through the Downs passes close by and there are several small barrows around its summit.

The accounts of Hackpen Hill as a fairy haunt are to be found in a work by the 17th-century antiquarian John Aubrey, who was born at Kington St Michael and pioneered the discipline of archaeology (he 'discovered' Avebury, for example), and who also made a study of local folklore and customs. A great deal of what we know today about Wiltshire's folklore comes from Aubrey's book *Remaines of Gentilisme and Judaisime*.

According to the stories Aubrey was told, people passing along the top of Hackpen Hill were in danger of being 'pixie-led'. This is to say, they would become unexpectedly lost in usually familiar surroundings or would find themselves wandering round and round in a daze, perhaps for hours. One man was 'led a dance' all the way to Devizes, coming out of his trance miles from home. Old charms against such a spell were to wear an item of clothing inside out or to carry a small cross of rowan wood. A shepherd was led underground by the fairies on Hackpen Hill, down into their own realm, where they entertained him by playing musical instruments, such as viols and lutes. He appears to have got away again unharmed.

However, Aubrey stated that, following their experiences, none of the men were able to 'afterwards enjoy themselves'. This suggests they suffered from melancholia after their experiences, a detail one sometimes finds in traditional accounts of people who have had an encounter with a ghost.

From Cricklade comes one other sighting of 'little people', but of much more recent date and with decidedly modern aspects. It can be found in the expertly compiled *Traveller's Guide to Fairy*

Sites by Janet Bord. Mrs Bord explains that the observers were two small boys, who were visiting the watercress beds in June 1977. She continues:

'Near an old hut by the cress beds they saw some little men "running about"; they were dressed in "red and yellow one-piece suits with air tanks on their backs" and had red eyes and helmets. "They ran very quickly with their knees up high." The boys were so frightened by what they saw that they climbed up a fallen tree, escaped on to the road and ran home.'

The presence of air tanks and one-piece suits makes one think of divers or astronauts and this strange yarn is often considered a 'close encounter' of the alien kind. But, as Mrs Bord points out, the diminutive beings' 'strange activity does sound in character for fairies' and she wonders 'whether what the boys saw (or thought they saw) was influenced by their cultural expectations'.

Once upon a time Hackpen Hill was considered a popular haunt of the fairies.

IStock Photo

WITCHES AND THE DARK ARTS

For many centuries it was believed that misfortune, illness and even death could be willed upon a person by another skilled in mystic arts or who had been given the power to do so by the Devil. Because witchcraft appears in the Bible (for example, in the story of the Witch of Endor and the conjuring up of a demon for King Solomon), the dark arts were believed in as firmly by educated people as the illiterate.

It might seem the height of foolish ignorance to believe in witchcraft but it should be remembered that, prior to the 18th century, almost nothing was understood about the causes of disease. Microbes were unknown. We believe in the virus giving us a cold even though we have never seen it, and our ancestors believed in the existence of witchcraft with the same degree of certainty.

So firm was the belief in witchcraft that someone accused of cursing an animal or human to fall ill or die was treated just the same as if they had poisoned or murdered their victims by more orthodox means. The criminal justice system saw no difference: the end result was all that mattered. By the dawn of the 17th century, however, Europe had fallen into the grip of a 'witch mania', fuelled in part by the resurgence of bubonic plague and by religious insecurity fanned by the Renaissance. No one was safe from being accused of being a witch. Lonely old women, especially those who had previously been known to provide herbal remedies, harmless love charms and the like, were early targets, but even the nobility found themselves accused, often by the unscrupulous as a means of getting them out of the way. Thousands of supposed witches and male sorcerers were hanged or burned alive as the mania swept Europe.

Unfortunately, Wiltshire was no exception. The witchtrials.co.uk website provides a list of those accused of witchcraft in the county during the 17th and early 18th centuries: 1613, Margaret Pilton; 1630, 'Goodwife' Barlowe; 1652, William Starr; 1653, Joan Baker, Elizabeth Beeman, Anne Bodenham, Joan Price; 1654, Elizabeth Loudon, Christiana Weekes; 1655, Margaret Gyngell; 1658, 'Widow' Orchard; 1665, Jane Mereweather; 1670, Elizabeth Peacock, Jane Townsend; 1672, Elizabeth Mills, Ann Tilling, Judith Witchell; 1685, Elizabeth Peacock, Ann Tilling, Judith Witchell (again!); 1687, M. Parle; 1689, Christiana Dunne, Margareta Young; 1698, Ruth Young; 1702, Joanna Tanner.

IStock Photo

An old engraving of witches' revels. Images like these propagated the fear of witchcraft throughout the 16th and 17th centuries.

Andrew and David Pickering put some flesh on the bones of some of these stats in their excellent book, *Witch-Hunting in England*. Here we learn that Anne Bodenham was especially notorious among her neighbours in the village of Fisherton Anger. At her trial, a Mr Mason testified that he visited Mrs Bodenham to gain some insight into a lawsuit he was engaged in. After paying his fee, he watched as Bodenham drew a circle on the floor with her staff and then placed a book of magic in its centre.

'After that,' said Mason, 'she laid a green glass on the book, and placed within the circle an earthen pot of coals wherein she threw something which caused a very noisome smell ... and so calling Beelzebub, Tormentor, Satan and Lucifer appear, there suddenly arose a very high wind which made the house shake. And presently, the back door flying open, there came five spirits ... in the likeness of ragged boys, some bigger than others, and ran about the house where she had drawn the staff; and the witch threw upon the ground crumbs of bread which the spirit picked up, and leaped often over the pan of coals in the midst of the circle, and a dog and cat of the witch's danced with him.'

This statement was originally quoted in a book published in 1688, *Kingdom of Darkness*, by Nicholas Crouch. The scene sounds like a piece of carefully managed stagecraft to me. Things became more serious, however, when Bodenham supplied arsenic to a woman who believed she was being poisoned by her daughters. The plot to kill the woman's daughters was exposed and the maidservant who had been tasked with buying the poison from Bodenham tried to save herself by claiming that the witch had made her make a pact with the Devil ... and so on.

It's probable a number of the other women listed above were simply 'wise women' practising rudimentary magic for a small fee. Christian

Weekes, of Cleeve Pepper, for example, specialised in finding stolen objects. Some, like Bodenham, conned their neighbours, but others no doubt believed in their powers and tried to be helpful.

The misdemeanours arising from the accounts collected by the Pickerings range from finger-pointing after a single unfortunate incident to a whole catalogue of supernatural persecutions. Joan Mereweather, of Bishops Cannings, was unfortunate enough to be accused of being a witch after kissing a baby, which shortly afterwards died. Jane Townsend, of Latton, and an unnamed woman of Devizes were separately accused of using 'poppets' – the old English version of voodoo dolls – to cause harm to others. Elizabeth Peacock, Judith Witchell, Anne Tilling and Elizabeth Mills were charged with belonging to a coven which cursed to death a young boy. Two were acquitted but two were hanged for the alleged crime.

The most colourful character was Widow Orchard of Malmesbury. Extraordinary tales were told about this redoubtable lady, who seemed to have the habit of going from door to door to beg for food. When refused, she would threaten to curse the householders. In one case, she was seen to pace out a circle outside the cottage of a girl who had earlier objected to giving her some scraps from her table. She sat in the middle of this circle and appeared to mumble an incantation. She repeated the procedure twice. Shortly afterwards the girl's hands seized up so that she was unable to use her fingers.

Goody Orchard, as she was also known, was immediately summonsed. In response to the accusation of witchcraft, she argued that the girl's crippled fingers must be due to her drinking bad water. Then she made a fatal mistake. She offered to cure her by bathing the girl's fingers in water while casting another spell.

The malady disappeared – and Goody Orchard was found guilty of practising witchcraft and was hanged at Salisbury.

Accounts of women – and occasionally men – being put on trial for practising witchcraft is clearly factual but the 'evidence' presented to condemn these unfortunates often reflects the folk beliefs of the time. In addition, there are several stories of Wiltshire witches which belong firmly in the realm of folklore. For example, Lyddie Shears never found herself on trial for witchcraft – she

Anne Bodenham divines the future with the help of dancing spirits and a pot of hot coals. The rather brazen young woman behind her may be intended to represent the maidservant whose purchase of poison led to Bodenham's downfall.

was fortunate to have lived in the 19th century – but the memory of her alleged powers lingered long into the 20th century. Unlike accounts such as those of Goody Orchard, it was wiser not to be kind to Lyddie than otherwise. She went round the neighbourhood of Winterslow selling oddments from a basket, but to buy them was dangerous, for they might put you under her spell (literally!).

Like many folkloric witches, Lyddie had an affinity with hares. The reason for this is obscure but may hark back to some pre-Christian superstition. Huntsmen would make gifts of tobacco to Lyddie in return for her using her craft to bring hares out of their coverts. She did this by striking flints against steel in order to make sparks, which attracted the animals. According to one local legend, however, she had an even more intimate relationship with hares – she was able to turn herself into one.

Lyddie enjoyed teasing a farmer named Tanner by adopting the guise of a hare when he was out coursing with his hounds. The hounds would chase after her and she would lead them a merry dance before vanishing away, leaving them and their master exhausted and frustrated. Finally, Farmer Tanner spotted the uncatchable hare disappearing into Lyddie Shears's garden. This arose certain dark suspicions in his mind and he told the rector all about it. This worthy gentlemen suggested Farmer Tanner get his hands on a silver bullet, a sure destroyer of witches, and shoot the hare with it. Tanner melted down a sixpence to make a bullet, which he then loaded into his gun.

The next time the hare appeared to tease his hounds, Farmer Tanner took aim and blasted the animal. The hare instantly vanished. Lyddie Shears also went unseen for a number of days until someone broke into her cottage to check on her. She was found, dead, with Farmer Tanner's silver bullet in her heart.

Witches were believed to have the ability to change into many things besides hares. A young man courting a girl from Potterne became unnerved by the sight of a greyhound which followed them wherever they went. He felt he and his girl were never really alone when they went out on one of their romantic rambles, for they would invariably glimpse the greyhound skulking around somewhere in the undergrowth, watching them. One evening, they decided to turn back early because it was wet. As they trudged homeward down the muddy lane, the suitor noticed the greyhound slinking ahead of them. It jumped over the garden gate and into the girl's cottage! The young man hurried to the house and found his girlfriend's mother in the kitchen washing mud off her legs. Ever afterwards he was convinced that their mysterious stalker had been his potential mother-in-law keeping an eye on them in greyhound form.

Perhaps one of the oddest alleged transformations occurs in an account of an incident that took place near Wootton Bassett in the 1860s. A man employed at Manor Farm was taking a cartload of corn to Devizes market when the leading horse of three suddenly stumbled and fell down dead. The other horses became frantic, as if terrified. Even after the dead beast had been uncoupled, the horses refused to go a step further along the road. Eventually, the carter had no choice but to turn around and head for home. The horses trotted along happily on the return journey.

The next day, the carter came to take away the body of the fallen horse. On its back he found something he hadn't noticed before: a thick piece of straw. He was later told by those versed in country lore that the straw was almost certainly a witch that had taken that form in order to cause the death of the horse. They added that if he had noticed it earlier and flogged the horse with it hard enough to draw blood, the curse would have been broken.

iStock Photo

Lyddie Shears, the Winterslow Witch, had a special affinity with hares and could even turn herself into one.

In the 1930s, Wiltshire author Ralph Whitlock was given an account of a curse placed upon Odstock Church by a Gypsy. This unique document was written down in the 19th century by the village blacksmith, Hiram Witt, who had been a witness to some of the events. Many years later Mr Whitlock devoted an entire chapter to 'The Odstock Curse' in his book on *The Folklore of Wiltshire*. In 1861, a Gypsy named Joshua Scamp was hanged for stealing a horse. The evidence against him was that his coat was found in the stable from which the horse was stolen. However, Joshua had missed his coat earlier that evening and it later came out that it had been taken by a younger man, Noah Lee. Because he was an old man, Joshua told his daughter that 'things were best left as they were'. When Lee was himself hanged not long afterwards for another crime, Joshua's daughter told her friends what her father had told her.

Touched by the tragedy, the Gypsies began an annual pilgrimage to Odstock churchyard to leave flowers on Joshua Scamp's grave. They also planted a tree by it. Years later, the vicar tried to stop the Gypsies from entering the churchyard and he ordered the tree they had planted as a memorial to be dug up. The Gypsies were understandably furious and a fight broke out. The police were called and the Gypsies forcibly evicted from the churchyard. The Gypsy queen was so angry that she pronounced a series of curses on those who had wronged her tribe.

She prophesied that in a year the vicar would be no longer able to preach; that the sexton who dug up the tree would die within a year; that the churchwarden would never have a son to inherit his farm; and that two 'turncoat' Gypsies who acted as special constables would die together and very soon. Having pronounced these curses, the Gypsy queen suddenly realised she had left her shawl behind in the church. Unfazed, she went to fetch it. But the church door was slammed in her face and locked. Angrier than ever, she pronounced a final curse: that whoever locked the church door again should die before the year was out.

All these pronouncements came true. The vicar developed a throat infection which prevented him from speaking and he died shortly after contracting it. The sexton did indeed die within a year. The churchwarden failed to sire a son and, worse still, all his cattle were destroyed by anthrax. What happened to the two brothers is a mystery: they vanished from the neighbourhood and were never heard of again. However, two skeletons, lying side by side, were many years later discovered lying in a shallow grave and it is thought these may have belonged to the hated traitors.

Validity was also placed on the curse the Gypsy queen placed on the church door. No one dared lock it. But in the year 1900 or

An old illustration of an English Gypsy queen. According to a unique document written down in the 19th century, a Wiltshire Gypsy queen wreaked a terrible revenge on the people who had abused her people in Odstock.

thereabouts a carpenter was hired to make a new pair of gates for the churchyard. The sexton warned him against locking the church door but the carpenter scoffed at the tale of the curse. There was no need for him to lock the door but he decided to anyway. The bolt had by this time become stiff with lack of use, but elbow grease soon had it dragged into place. The door was now locked for the first time in decades. Soon after, the sexton was passing the cottage where the carpenter was lodging and heard moans and groans coming from within. He found the man doubled up in pain. Soon he was transferred to hospital. And there he died. The church door was unbolted.

In the 1930s, when the then rector went on his annual holiday, his locum decided to lock the door, scorning what he considered unseemly superstition on the part of the incumbent. He too died within the year. On returning from his holiday, the rector unlocked the door and threw the key into the River Ebble. In 1976, when his work on Wiltshire folklore was published, Ralph Whitlock was still able to confidently assert: 'The church door at Oldstock is never locked.' According to Jacqueline Simpson and Jennifer Westwood's magnum opus on English folklore, *The Lore of the Land*, this state of affairs continued until the early 1990s, when the Bishop of Ramsbury held a service to lift the curse. Now the door is sometimes locked, 'when safety requires'.

CHURCH AND CLERGY

Salisbury Cathedral really is a wonder. It was built in the 13th century and is a splendid example of the Early English Gothic style of architecture. It has the tallest spire of any church in Britain. It also has the largest cloisters and the largest close of any English cathedral. Moreover, it contains the world's oldest working clock and the best preserved copy of the *Magna Carta*.

The cathedral's setting among beautiful water meadows was said to have been chosen thanks to the intervention of the Virgin Mary. A much older building served as a cathedral in Old Sarum, an ancient enclosure outside the modern city. This location was considered too cramped and inconvenient, but the building of a new cathedral was hampered by the then bishop, Richard Poore, being unable to find a more suitable site. The Virgin appeared to the bishop and told him to build it in the 'Maer-field'. He'd never heard of such a place but a few days later overheard some men referring to the Maer-field. He at once ordered the work to start in this field. Salisbury Cathedral is dedicated to the Virgin Mary.

Among the other traditions of the cathedral is the one relating to a small, worn statue of a bishop, wearing a gown and mitre and carrying a crozier. It was discovered in 1680 and its size immediately suggested to some people that it represented a Boy Bishop. There was a custom carried out in England and elsewhere to choose one among the boys in the choir to serve a spell as a sort of mini-bishop. The custom was adopted in Salisbury Cathedral for a time, too.

Soon after it was found, a story became current to explain the presence of the effigy. It told of a youngster chosen to become a Boy Bishop who was prone to melancholy. One day, the boy was so down in the dumps that his friends jumped on him and tried to cheer him up by tickling him. Unfortunately, they overdid it – and tickled him to death! Because he was still 'in office', as it were, the poor little chap was buried in his robes and with the full honours that might be expected of a grown-up bishop. Today it is generally considered that the effigy's smallness has nothing to do with the person it originally commemorated: it probably belonged at one time to a larger memorial.

Another legend tells of a bishop of Salisbury Cathedral who died abroad in the year 1414. While his body was lying in state, a great flock of unknown white birds flew out of the sky and settled on the roof. They made quite a clamour all night and no one recalled ever having seen anything quite like them before. From then on, states the tradition, mysterious white birds will be seen in the vicinity of the cathedral whenever its incumbent bishop is about to die.

The tradition may have started as recently as 1885, for it was in that year that the then bishop's daughter, Annie Moberley, saw two white birds flap out of the palace gardens while her father lay dying. The author Edith Olivier, herself a keen collector of Wiltshire folklore, claimed to have had a similar experience in 1911. She saw two 'very large white birds' soaring across a neighbouring meadow on the day the bishop died. Stranger still, the birds were flying without moving their wings.

The subject of flying leads us neatly on to the Benedictine monastic house at Malmesbury. Malmesbury Abbey was founded as long ago as the 7th century and King Athelstan is buried here. It grew in size and importance during the medieval period and was widely

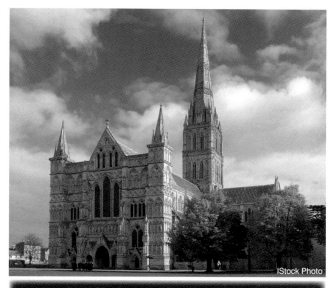

Spectacular Salisbury Cathedral boasts a number of interesting old traditions.

regarded as a centre of learning. By the 11th century it boasted the largest library in Europe. About the year 1125 one of its scholar monks, William of Malmesbury, published a book called *Deeds of the English Kings*, which remains an essential history for scholars of the Anglo-Saxon period. In it William mentions the extraordinary adventure of a flying monk at Malmesbury.

According to William, a monk called Elmer 'had hazarded an attempt of singular temerity' as a young man. He continues: 'He had by some contrivance fastened wings to his hands and feet, in order that, looking upon the fable as true, he might fly like Daedalus; and collecting the air on the summit of a tower, had flown for more than the distance of a furlong; but, agitated by the violence of the wind and the current of air, he fell and broke both his legs, and was lame ever after. He used to relate as the cause of his failure, his forgetting to provide himself with a tail.'

Whether the story is true or not is now open to conjecture. It is probably an old folk tale, following a long tradition that started with the Ancient Greek myth of Daedalus and the ill-fated Icarus, which William refers to. However, it seems likely that people did experiment with manned flight from time to time and it's possible that Elmer did so and was more successful than most. At any rate, the putative flying monk is commemorated in a stained glass window in Malmesbury Abbey.

The abbey was founded by St Aldhelm, who had a reputation for magical feats. He once trapped a flock of birds in a roofless barn to stop them eating the abbey's grain. When the abbey was under construction, he threw his glove on the ground and told the masons that where it fell they would find treasure. The greedy men hastily dug up the ground, and uncovered a seam of ideal building stone. One of the abbey's bells is named after St Aldhelm. It is said to have the power to drive away storms when rung.

Malmesbury Abbey suffered under Henry VIII's Dissolution of the Monasteries but the church survives as a place of worship and the ruins and gardens are well worth a visit.

The church in the village of Bishopstrow is dedicated to St Aldhelm. Here, according to William of Malmesbury, the magical saint planted his staff in the ground and it grew into an ash tree, which in turn multiplied into a grove of ash trees. 'Bishopstrow' supposedly means 'Bishop's Tree' but, as Simpson and Westwood point out, the Old English word *treow* also translates as a large wooden cross and the name more likely refers to a preaching cross that stood here before the church was built.

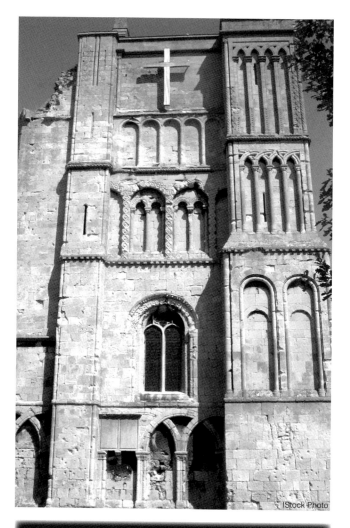

A medieval monk is said to have jumped from one of Malmesbury Abbey's towers in an early attempt at manned flight.

A carving over the doorway of Little Langford Church appears to show this miracle of St Aldhelm. It is of a man in a robe standing beside a leafy tree with birds sitting in it. A much weirder local tradition is attached to this sculpture, however. It is said a girl once found a maggot in a nut and decided, for some bizarre reason, to make a pet of it. She fed the maggot until it grew into a monster. Eventually it killed her and then went rogue in the local woods, before being hunted down and destroyed by the villagers. The sculpture is sometimes known as 'The Maid and the Maggot', the bishop supposedly representing the maid and his crozier the monster.

Peculiar traditions belong to numerous Wiltshire churches. Purton, for example, is the only one in the county to feature two spires. One is at the west end, the other in the centre. The story goes that the church was being built with money provided by two sisters. They couldn't agree on how they wanted the church to look so a compromise was reached in which each got the spire they wanted. In fact, the two spires were raised at periods 150 years apart, so this is clearly just a local legend.

At St John the Baptist's in Stockton, the gravestone of Ann Raxworthy, who died 1829, has been laid in the path so everyone entering the church has to tread on it. Ann was supposedly a lady's maid who, on her retirement, dressed way beyond her social station – according to the views of the time – when she came to church services. Good on her, say I, but on her deathbed Ann felt so guilty over this harmless show of vanity that she insisted on the humiliating placing of her grave as an act of penance.

Inside the church of St Peter ad Vincula, Broad Hinton, can be found a rather more splendid memorial. The Elizabethan marble tomb commemorates Sir Thomas Wroughton, Lady Wroughton and their seven children with well-executed statues. Unfortunately, the memorial has been vandalised, probably during the Civil War when Parliamentarian soldiers went around smashing anything they considered too elaborate or 'Popish'. The piously praying hands of Sir Thomas and the seven children have all been knocked off. Only

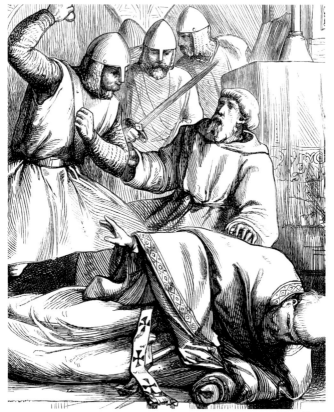

IStock Photo

Thomas Becket's murder in Canterbury Cathedral. Local lore has it that Becket served as a curate in Wiltshire and several tales are told about him.

Lady Wroughton's effigy has been spared, probably because she is represented as holding a Bible.

A strange tale has built up around this damaged tomb. It states that Sir Thomas and his wife had opposing religious views: he was a Catholic, she was a Protestant. One day, Sir Thomas came home to find Lady Wroughton reading her Bible instead of getting his dinner ready, and in a temper he threw the Good Book into the fire. Lady Wroughton rescued it, but badly burned her hands in doing so. Godly retribution then fell on Sir Thomas. His hands dropped off and all his children were born handless.

Wiltshire also has a number of traditions about Thomas Becket, the Archbishop of Canterbury whose public rows with King Henry II led to his assassination in 1170. Becket was canonised after his murder in Canterbury Cathedral and a significant religious cult grew up around him. There is a story of a young boy who met on Salisbury Plain two tall, stately men carrying a bowl. They explained to the wondering child that the bowl was full of the blood of St Thomas of Canterbury. Then they vanished.

Another tradition has it that the young Becket served as curate of Winterbourne Earls. He had a favourite walk from the village to Clarendon Park and in after years the route trodden by his sacred feet had become a mysterious track, only visible from a distance, and on which no vegetation would grow and which snow would never cover. It was called St Thomas Becket's Path. Rather more secular is the amusing yarn which states that every year the Archbishop would come to the village fair at Crockerton but would always leave in rags, having spent or gambled away all his money!

FOOLS, HEROES AND VILLAINS

One of Wiltshire's best-known legends and one that has gained a wide currency is that of the Moonrakers. This time-worn yarn tells of some men riding through a Wiltshire village in the middle of the night and noticing a small group of 'rustics' gathered round a pond. The countrymen were poking under the water with long-handled hay-rakes. The horsemen asked them what they were up to at that time of night and received the reply: 'Why, we be a-raking for thicky gurt big cheese wot be fallen in our pond.'

They pointed to the moon's reflection in the pond. The strangers laughed at the yokels' stupidity at mistaking the moon for a round of cheese and rode on their way. Once they were out of sight, the villagers went back to what they were really doing – raking up barrels of smuggled brandy which they had hidden in the pond. The horsemen were the true fools, for they were excisemen, tasked with seeking out contraband goods.

This tale has been told about a number of places, but the best-known location is a pool called the Crammer, on the outskirts of Devizes. The word 'Moonraker' became a nickname for Wiltshire men in general, even though the story was later claimed for locations outside the county. Recently, I heard a stand-up comic repeat a version in which he claimed to have seen drunks on a night out in a northern town trying to fish the moon's reflection out of a puddle, in the belief that it was a pound coin. Bowdlerized versions of the tale often miss out the true cunning of the apparent bumpkins.

Rivalry between communities in rural Britain created a number of examples of folk tales intended to show the stupidity of neighbouring villagers. The Moonrakers story may well have started off in this way, with the locals later flipping it into a tale of their own cleverness. A common trope in such stories is the failure to recognise something quite ordinary and to imbue it with a terrible importance. In Cheshire, for example, the people of Stanney were supposedly terrified of a duck which had the habit of waddling around the lanes after dark. After a 'brave' soul claimed to have waylaid the harmless creature and chopped off its head, the villagers became even more afraid of it, assuming it to be a ghost.

Another yarn with a wildfowl theme used to be told about the people of Aldbourne. The villagers became alarmed at the sight of something strange swimming round the duck pond. The worried yokels scratched their heads and puzzled over the creature until one bright spark suggested sending for the oldest person in the village, since he may have seen such a thing in his long experience. This elderly fellow was so feeble, he had to be brought to the pond in a wheelbarrow. The patriarch was pushed three times round the pond so he could get a good look at the mysterious visitor. Only then was he able to identify it as a dabchick, a small and inoffensive bird. Villagers from Aldbourne were ever afterwards called 'dabchicks' by their neighbours. For many years rivals displayed dead dabchicks to annoy the Aldbourne team during inter-village sporting matches.

Another case of mistaken identity was told about Bishops Cannings. The story was recorded for posterity by a contributor to the *Wiltshire Archaeological and Natural History Magazine* in 1943. It is quoted in Ralph Whitlock's *The Folklore of Wiltshire*:

'A shepherd coming home to dinner one day saw on the downs above Cannings a large watch. He had never seen a watch before, and being

An old postcard sold in Devizes bore this illustration of the Moonrakers legend.

afraid of the thing, thinking it was something dangerous as he could hear it ticking very loudly, he hurried to the village and told the sexton "there were a great ugly beast up on the downs, and would he come and see it". The sexton was a fat, heavy man and said he could not walk so far, but persuaded a couple of the villagers to wheel him up in a wheelbarrow. Two of them had their spades in their hands, and putting these in the wheelbarrow with the sexton they made their way up to the spot, guided by the shepherd.

'On approaching the site they stopped and listened to the ticking of the watch. The sexton then said, "Mates, just wheel I round him," which was done. "Now wheel I round him again," and this was done a third time, when the sexton said, "Mates, chuck I out," and crawling up nearer the "beast" and listening for a minute he exclaimed, "Mates, it be a dangerous ticktoad, so smash him up." Whereupon the men with the spades smashed the watch and dug a hole and buried the pieces.'

This story is another which features the supposed wise man being paraded around the object of concern three times in a wheelbarrow. This detail crops up in similar stories from around the UK; it's an irresistibly absurd image, the rustic equivalent of a grand man in his carriage.

Nor is the tale of the 'ticktoad' the only one highlighting the alleged stupidity of the people of Bishops Cannings. Another tells of the building of the church, which initially, so the story goes, had two spires. One was much shorter than the other, however (possibly a reference to a small lantern tower built on to the spire). Neighbouring villagers ridiculed the builders for this. Nothing daunted, the Bishops Cannings folk vowed to help the smaller spire grow – by heaping up manure around its base. When the manure began to sink into the ground, the dimwits mistook this for the spire getting taller and crowed over their achievement.

The villagers of Downton also found themselves the butt of a number of tall tales about their lack of common sense. One story has them capturing a cuckoo, that iconic harbinger of summer, and imprisoning it in the pound. In this way, they thought, they would preserve summer in the village all year long. This yarn may have been suggested by Downton's 'Cuckoo Fair', their annual spring fair which was held on St George's Day (23 April). Another has them removing an eel from a pond because it was killing their fish and throwing it into another pond, thinking that it would drown there. The Moonrakers story is also told about the people of Downton.

In addition to these tales about anonymous country bumpkins, there are others about much more notable characters. Alfred the Great, the 9th-century king of Wessex who finally defeated the invading Danes in the face of almost insurmountable odds, has

According to one rather disparaging story, the appearance of a tiny dabchick on the pond at Aldbourne caused alarm among the dimwitted villagers.

a strong link to Wiltshire. The decisive battle against the invaders took place at 'Ethandun' in 878, identified as the village of Edington, near Westbury. There are numerous traditions about King Alfred in the neighbourhood of Edington. One of these is the famous story of the burning of the cakes.

According to the legend, King Alfred was engaged in guerrilla warfare with the marauding Norsemen, moving through the countryside in small bands, keeping under cover and striking when they could. Somewhere near Brixton Deverill, the bedraggled and exhausted king took shelter in a peasant's cottage. The poor man and his wife let him stay, but were unaware of his identity. After a day or so's rest, Alfred had got his strength back and was able to contemplate his next move against the Danes.

The woman of the house asked him to watch over some cakes she was cooking on the griddle, but so absorbed was he in his strategies that he forgot about them and they were burned. The woman was very angry and scolded her monarch for his neglect. Some say she even beat him with a stick. The king was contrite, even amused, by this incident and it reminded him of the importance of always keeping alert. He did not reveal his regal identity but left that day to continue the war, which ultimately he won. (Another version of the tale places the events at Athelney, King Alfred's last stronghold in the Somersetshire marshes.)

Other traditions local to Edington are that Alfred slept under an oak tree on the downs the night before the Battle of Ethandun; that his army assembled by two standing stones opposite Kingston Deverill Church; and that six springs now in the grounds of Stourhead House appeared miraculously when the king prayed for something to drink.

Also nearby is the Westbury White Horse, carved into the hillside on Bratton Down. Some believe that the original of this horse was created in the chalk to celebrate the Battle of Ethandun. The current horse was made in 1778, exactly 900 years after this decisive battle.

King Alfred burns the cakes. One version of this time-worn tradition places the event in Wiltshire.

Another early monarch to feature in Wiltshire tradition is Athelstan. In his *Remaines of Gentilisme and Judaisme*, John Aubrey relates a tradition that the 10th-century king was passing along the Fosse Way, a Roman road, through Newnton when he noticed a peasant woman beside the road. She was sitting on a stool, to which a cow was tethered, grazing on the grass on the verge. This struck Athelstan as a highly inconvenient way of grazing a cow: the woman was unable to move from the stool and the cow only had a limited amount of grass to chomp on. He asked her about it and she explained that there was no common land thereabouts where a cow could be left to graze. The queen listened in and agreed that it was a shame that Newnton should have no common land.

It so happened that the land adjoining the highway had been donated by Athelstan to a nearby monastery, and the king decided that they could spare a bit of it. So, rather bizarrely, he told the woman to get up on a horse without a saddle and to ride it round the field. The area she succeeded in covering before either getting too sore or falling off was then marked out and donated as common land for the people of Newnton.

A decade or two after Athelstan's reign, the Danes were back wreaking havoc in England and a new hero arose in Wiltshire, by the name of John Rattlebone. It is uncertain whether Rattlebone ever existed in real life; his name would suggest not but, like Robin Hood, King Arthur and other legendary heroes, it's just possible that he does represent a folk memory of a real person or incident.

The incident that defines the legend of John Rattlebone took place during a scrap with the Danes, possibly in the year 1016. This mighty warrior was in the thick of battle when an enemy's sword sliced through his stomach, nearly disembowelling him. Such a blow would have put paid to most men, but Rattlebone snatched up a tile he saw lying on the ground and pressed it to the wound. With one hand using the tile to hold in his guts and the other still swinging his sword, Rattlebone fought on to help the English to victory. He survived the battle, the wound healing, and he was granted land in Sherston and in nearby hamlets. These spoils were recorded in a locally remembered rhyme, quoted by the ubiquitous John Aubrey:

> 'Fight well Rattlebone,
> Thou shalt have Sherstone.'
> 'What shall I with Sherstone doe
> Without I have all that belongs thereto?'
> 'Thou shalt have Wyck & Willesly,
> Easton towne and Pinkeney.'

The existence of John Rattlebone may have been suggested by a weathered statue in the porch of Sherston Church, which looked like it might have been of a knight clutching a shield or tile to his stomach. Originally, it was probably intended to represent a monk with a Bible. For many years its ambiguous appearance allowed it to be proudly pointed out as a statue of Rattlebone.

It's possible John Rattlebone existed but it is highly unlikely that our next Wiltshire worthy is anything other than mythical. Merlin, the greatest wizard of them all (even Gandalf would have tipped his pointy hat to him), is supposedly buried in Marlborough. Merlin's origins date back to ancient Welsh texts, in which he is called Myrddyn. Geoffrey of Monmouth, the important 12th-century chronicler, renamed him Merlin and he became associated with King Arthur.

The name Marlborough is the modern form of an Old English name meaning 'the mound of Maerla'. The mound is probably the one in the grounds of the town's famous public school. It is unknown who 'Maerla' was but he was identified with Merlin as long ago as the 13th century. A strong desire for the mythical wizard to belong to Marlborough continued well into the 19th century, when one author placed under the arms of the town the Latin phrase 'Ubi nunc sapientis ossa Merlini?' ('Where now are the bones of wise Merlin?')

The only other tradition connecting Merlin to Wiltshire is, as we saw in the first chapter, that he built Stonehenge. We know nothing else of his supposed activities in the county, nor does one exist regarding his death and burial in Marlborough. Perhaps the link was merely scholarly wishful thinking.

Does Marlborough's name really refer to the burial place of the wizard Merlin?

The flipside of the heroic figures to be found in Wiltshire's legendary lore are the rogues and criminals. A number of highwaymen were long recalled in fireside tales. One of the best known was Thomas Boulter. Boulter had a horse named Black Bess, a name later given to Dick Turpin's horse by writers of romances. Turpin's best-known fictional feat was riding from London to York in a single night. The real Black Bess managed an impressive ride, too: eighty miles from Windsor to Boulton's home in Poulshot. Boulton was an unusual highwayman, quietly spoken, always polite to his victims, and rather timid. Before he became a robber he ran a ladies' hat shop. His career came to an end when he was hanged in 1778.

Two other Wiltshire 'gentlemen of the road' were the sons of clergymen. One of these, James Whitney, was the son of the rector of Donhead St Andrew. His gang once stole the mighty sum of £15,000 from just one stagecoach but they too ended their lives on the gallows. There was even a lady highwaywoman, a Mary Sandall, of Baverstock, but she succeeded in only stealing two shillings and a cloak before she was apprehended.

Beside the road from Devizes to Salisbury there is a monument commemorating a robbery that took place in 1839. A Mr Dean, who ran a farm at the now abandoned village of Imber, was held up by four highwaymen on the evening of 21 October, but this was just the start of the drama. There then followed a three-hour chase which was so intense that one of the crooks fell down dead. The other three were caught. The memorial's inscription reads: 'This monument is erected by public subscription as a warning to those who presumptuously think to escape the punishment God has threatened against Thieves and Robbers.'

A romantic elaboration of this adventure was told to Ralph Whitlock. It makes out Mr Dean as a quick-witted hero (perhaps it was he who put the story about?). According to this version of events, the victim turned the table on his assailants by proposing a wager.

'I bet', he said, 'that I'm a better shot than any of you lot. We'll throw my hat in the air, and the one who puts more holes in it before it touches the ground takes the money.'

The robbers agreed, and everyone blasted away at the hat. The impact of the bullets kept the hat in the air for some time. Then all went quiet as one of the highwaymen said: 'Wait a bit, the pistols are empty.'

'Mine isn't,' laughed the triumphant Mr Dean. 'Hands up!'

Another tradition of dark wrongdoings was recorded by Kathleen Wiltshire. She heard tales of a sinister inn with the deceptively friendly name of the Shepherd and Dog. It once stood near Lydeway but after its grim secret was uncovered, it was abandoned and later pulled down. It transpired that the landlord of this lonely wayside inn had fitted a trapdoor into the floor. He would select suitable victims, such as merchants travelling alone, and would use the trapdoor to propel them into the cellar, where he would rob and murder them. After killing untold numbers of people in this way, one of his victims, a pedlar, survived the drop and managed to get away. The landlord was arrested and the cellar floor dug up, revealing shallow graves crammed with bodies.

There are a number of tales of highwaymen up to no good on Wiltshire's roads.

iStock Photo

SWAIN SC

WILD WILL DARRELL

The greatest villain featured in Wiltshire folklore must surely be William Darrell, known as 'Wild Will'. He earns this reputation from just one deed, but a terrible one it was. Darrell was the squire of Littlecote Hall during the reign of the first Elizabeth. Littlecote only just belongs to Wiltshire: it is right on the border with Berkshire. This magnificent country house is now a hotel.

The legend of Littlecote is something of a horror story. Nevertheless, there exists documentary evidence to suggest that the incidents – most of them anyway – have a basis in historical fact. Now follows the tale as related by John Ingram in his seminal work on *Haunted Homes and Family Legends*:

'It was on a dark rainy night in the month of November, that an old midwife sat musing by her cottage fireside, when on a sudden she was startled by a loud knocking at the door. On opening it, she found a horseman, who told her that her assistance was required immediately by a person of rank, and that she should be handsomely rewarded, but there were reasons for keeping the affair a strict secret and she must therefore submit to being blind-folded, and to be conducted in that condition to the bed-chamber of a lady. With some hesitation the midwife consented; the horseman bound her eyes, and placed her on a pillion behind him.

'After proceeding in silence for many miles, through rough and dirty lanes, they stopped, and the midwife was led into a house which, from the length of her walk through the apartments, as well as the sounds about her, she discovered to be the seat of power.

When the bandage was removed from her eyes, she found herself in a bed-chamber, in which was the lady on whose account she had been sent for, and a man of haughty and ferocious aspect.

'The lady was delivered of a fine boy. Immediately, the man commanded the midwife to give him the child, and, catching it from her, he hurried across the room and threw it on the back of the fire that was blazing in the chimney. The child, however, was strong, and by its struggles rolled itself off upon the hearth, when the ruffian again seized it with fury, and, in spite of the intercession of the midwife, and the more piteous entreaties of the mother, thrust it under the grate, and, raking the live coals upon it, soon put an end to its life.

'The midwife, after spending some time in affording all the relief in her power to the wretched mother, was told that she must be gone. Her former conductor appeared, who again bound her eyes, and conveyed her behind him to her own home; he then paid her handsomely and departed. The midwife was strongly agitated by the horrors of the preceding night, and she immediately made a deposition of the facts before a magistrate. Two circumstances afforded hopes of detecting the house in which the crime had been committed; one was, that the midwife, as she sat by the bed-side, had, with a view to discover the place, cut out a piece of the bed-curtain, and sewn it in again; the other was, that as she had descended the staircase she had counted the steps.

'Some suspicion fell upon one Darrell, at the time the proprietor of Littlecote House and the domain around it. The house was examined, and identified by the midwife, and Darrell was tried at Salisbury for the murder. By corrupting his judge, he escaped the sentence of the law, but broke his neck by a fall from his horse in hunting, a few months afterwards. The place where this happened is still known [at least as late as 1912] as Darrell's Stile – a spot to be dreaded by the peasant whom the shades of evening have overtaken on his way.'

According to some versions of the story, Darrell's accident was no accident but vengeance from beyond the grave. An apparition of the murdered baby, wreathed in flames, appeared on the path, startling his horse, which reared and threw him. According to John Ingram, Littlecote also became haunted after the tragedy. He writes: 'The apparition of a woman with dishevelled hair, in white garments, and bearing a babe in her arm, haunts the gloomy chamber [where the child was murdered].'

There are many more tales of haunted houses in Wiltshire, and these will be explored in a forthcoming book of *Wiltshire Ghost Stories* to be published by Bradwell Books later in the year. We have room here, however, for one more spooky story that has passed into legend.

The bedroom in Littlecote Hall which features in the legend of Wild Will Darrell.

THE DEMON DRUMMER

'The Demon Drummer of Tedworth' is considered a classic of English ghost-lore but at the time the events allegedly took place (the 1660s) it was widely believed they were caused by witchcraft. One or two people blamed the fairies. It is arguably the most extraordinary story Wiltshire has to offer.

Today Tedworth is spelled Tidworth. It is situated on the eastern edge of Salisbury Plain and is a garrison town, just as it was in the 17th century. As a military centre, it used to attract discharged or retired soldiers who were down on their luck. They hoped to extract a few coins from people who might feel more sympathy for their plight than others. In March 1661, a former military drummer of the name of William Drury arrived in Tidworth. Morning, noon and night Drury would play noisy tattoos to literally drum up business and he soon became a nuisance. He had a pass giving him permission to play his drum in public places but unluckily for him, one of the magistrates, John Mompesson, knew well the two dignitaries who had supposedly signed it and he recognised the signatures as forgeries. Drury was locked up in the town gaol pending further inquiries. He begged that he should be allowed to keep his drum but it was impounded.

What happened next is rather confused but it seems the constable took pity on Drury and let him go, but did not return his drum, presumably so he could no longer create a nuisance. Unsure what to do with the drum, he forwarded it to Mr Mompesson's house.

This is when things got peculiar. Mr Mompesson had been away from home, but when he returned, his wife told him that for three nights running the house was disturbed by 'a great knocking' on the doors and external walls. It was if a gang of thieves had been trying to break in.

This was just the beginning. According to a contemporary account (*Saducismus Triumphatus* by Joseph Glanvill): 'After this the noise of thumping and drumming was very frequent, usually five nights together, and then it would intermit three. It was on the outside of the house, which is most of it of board. It constantly came as they were going to sleep, whether early or late.'

After a month of this the noises began to be heard in the room where Drury's drum had been stashed. Before the sounds began, the household would detect 'a hurling in the air over the house'. The clear beat of a drum would emerge out of the general cacophony just before it ceased. The entire duration of the phenomena was for about two hours a night. After two months, the pregnant Mrs Mompesson was 'brought to bed' in order to give birth to her child. During this period, and for a few weeks after the birth, the knockings were not heard and the household began to think they had heard the last of the phenomenon.

'But after this civil cessation,' writes Glanvill, 'it returned in a ruder manner than before.' Now the 'Demon Drummer' began to make a target of the children in the house, in the way poltergeists are often said to do. It drummed out recognisable rhythms on their bedsteads but with such violence everyone expected them to fall apart. Scratching sounds would also be heard. The drumming would pursue children from room to room. The spirit, or whatever it was, disturbed prayers by throwing around chairs, shoes 'and every loose thing', and even struck the minister on the leg, though

An illustration of the Demon Drummer of Tedworth, from the frontispiece of the book which brought the phenomenon to the attention of the public, Saducismus Triumphatus, by Joseph Glanvill. The author experienced the Demon Drummer's activity for himself.

very gently. One morning, 'it left a sulphurous smell behind it, which was very offensive'. Devilish indeed! The children were moved out to a lodging house. But the disturbances did not stop.

At this point in the narrative, Glanvill makes a few interesting asides. He points out that some of the sounds made by the entity were so loud that they could be heard 'at a considerable distance in the fields'. Nevertheless, dogs about the house were unmoved by them, although one might have expected them to be particularly sensitive. He also notes a conversation Mr Mompesson's mother had with a neighbour. The neighbour mentioned a belief that fairies had a habit of leaving money, to which the other lady replied that if they did so it would at least 'make amends for their trouble'. Clearly, the two women considered fairies might be responsible for the noises. (This little snippet also goes some way to confirming my assumption that fairies were indeed part of folk belief in Wiltshire despite the lack of stories about them.)

However, in most people's opinion the phenomena were being caused, through some supernatural agency, by William Drury, whose drum now lay in the house. One night, a number of men of rank joined the Mompessons to experience the 'Demon Drummer' for themselves. One of them called out: 'Satan, if the drummer set the work, give three knocks, and no more.' Three distinct knocks were then heard. He then asked, as further confirmation that Drury was behind the disturbances, to knock five more times, but then to stop for the rest of the night. Five more knocks came and then no more.

Adding fuel to the belief that the disturbances were of demonic origin, one morning a Bible was found on the ashes of the fire, unharmed despite lying open and paper-side down. It lay open at a chapter in Mark's Gospel, where there is mention made of Christ giving his disciples the power to cast out devils.

As the haunting – or curse, or whatever it was – continued, things grew even stranger. It began to make a noise like a big dog panting. Servants would be thrown out of bed or would feel a great weight on top of them. Mysterious lights were seen about the house, including one, blue in colour, which 'caused great stiffness in the eyes of those that saw it' (I'm not quite sure what this means, but it's most intriguing). Rooms would suddenly become hot or full of a sweet, disgusting scent. On one occasion, Mr Mompesson's servant spread ashes on the floor of his bed-chamber, to ensure no one was entering it after dark. The next morning letters, circles and other weird symbols were found scratched into the ashes and, most alarming of all, claw marks.

Finally, the entity began to speak. By this time Joseph Glanvill had himself arrived on the scene to help investigate the strange goings-on. He had already heard the usual knocks and scratches for himself and with a friend had thoroughly poked about the various rooms in a vain search for a cause. He wrote: 'We could discover nothing; so that I was verily persuaded, and am so still, that the noise was made by some demon or spirit.'

In the midst of a round of knocking, Glanvill asked the empty room, 'In the name of God, who is it, and what would you have?' A disembodied voice replied, 'Nothing of you.'

On another occasion a voice cried out in the children's bedroom, 'A witch! A witch!' It continued to yell this frightening but puzzling word over a hundred times, according to Glanvill. One might imagine that things could get no weirder. But they did. Seeing some wood moving in the hearth, Mr Mompesson fired his pistol at it. The wood stopped moving but drops of blood appeared in the hearth. Others were found on the stairs, as if something invisible had been injured and had crawled away. Apparitions began to be seen. A servant was terrified by a 'great body' looming over his bed, in which were set two 'red and glaring' eyes. Groups of manlike shapes were seen to shuffle about the house but could be frightened away by discharging a pistol.

So, at last, we come to the man accused of causing all this chaos: William Drury. It took two years to track him down, but eventually he was arrested in Gloucester for stealing and he was locked in the town gaol. There he met a man from Wiltshire and asked for news of his home county. The reply was that there was no news. At this the drummer became annoyed.

'No!' he allegedly said. 'Do not you hear of the drumming at a gentleman's house at Tedworth?'

'That I do enough,' replied his fellow prisoner.

'I have plagued him,' Drury said, 'and he shall never be quiet till he hath made me satisfaction for taking away my drum.'

Drury now found himself accused of witchcraft. His trial was held at Salisbury and he was sentenced to transportation. During his trial and absence from England, the disturbances at Tidworth ceased. When he found himself back on English soil, they began again. In the meantime, his alleged victim, Mr Mompesson, found his reputation seriously tarnished. As Glanvill puts it: 'The unbelievers in the matter of spirits and witches took him for an impostor. Many others judged the permission of such an extraordinary evil to be the judgement of God upon him, for some notorious wickedness or impiety.'

Glanvill stands by him, however, and his account of the Demon Drummer of Tedworth ends with the following conclusion: 'I answer that there are divers particulars in the story in which no abuse or deceit could have been practised; as the motion of boards and chairs of themselves; the beating of a drum in the midst of the room and in the air when nothing was to be seen; the great heat in a chamber which had no fire in excessive cold weather; the scratching and panting, the violent beating and shaking of the bedsteads, of which there was no perceivable cause or occasion; in these and such like instances, it is not to be conceived how tricks could have been put upon so many.'

IStock Photo

A Victorian representation of the Demon Drummer,
now reimagined as a ghost wandering Salisbury Plain.

ALSO FROM RICHARD HOLLAND FOR BRADWELL BOOKS

LEGENDS & FOLKLORE
Nottinghamshire
Scottish
Wales

GHOST STORIES
Cambridgeshire
Cheshire
Cotswolds
Cumbrian
Dorset
Essex
Hampshire & the Isle of Wight
Kent
Lancashire
London
Norfolk
North Wales
Oxfordshire
Scottish
Somerset
South Wales
Surrey
Sussex
Yorkshire

BY OTHER AUTHORS
Black Country & Birmingham
(Brendan Hawthorne)
Cornish (A Corn)
Derbyshire (Jill Armitage)
Leicestershire (David Bell)

London Underground (Jill
Armitage)
Staffordshire (David Bell)
Welsh Celebrity Ghost Stories
(South Wales Paranormal
Research)

FROM RICHARD HOLLAND IN 2015/16

LEGENDS & FOLKLORE
Cambridgeshire
Hampshire
Dorset
Somerset

GHOST STORIES
Dorset
Herefordshire
Norfolk
Shropshire
Somerset
Warwickshire
Northumberland
Nottinghamshire
Devon
Lincolnshire

For more information visit
www.bradwellbooks.com